CRABTREE
CONTACT

SPACE
SURVIVAL GUIDE

Ruth Owen

🌴 Crabtree Publishing Company

www.crabtreebooks.com

Crabtree Publishing Company

www.crabtreebooks.com   1-800-387-7650

PMB 59051   616 Welland Avenue,
350 Fifth Avenue, 59th Floor   St. Catharines, Ontario
New York, NY, 10118   L2M 5V6

Content development by   Published by
Shakespeare Squared   Crabtree Publishing
                               Company © 2010
www.ShakespeareSquared.com
                               First published
No part of this publication may   in Great Britain in
be reproduced, copied, stored in 2010 by TickTock
a retrieval system or transmitted in Entertainment Ltd.
any form or by any means electronic,
mechanical, photocopying, recording   Printed in the
or otherwise without prior written   U.S.A./122009
permission of the copyright owner.   CG20091120

Crabtree Publishing Company
credits:
Project manager: Kathy Middleton
Editor: Reagan Miller
Proofreader: Crystal Sikkens
Production coordinator: Katherine Berti
Prepress technician: Katherine Berti

TickTock credits:
Publisher: Melissa Fairley
Art director: Faith Booker
Editor: Emma Dods
Designer: Emma Randall
Production controller: Ed Green
Production manager: Suzy Kelly

Thank you to Lorraine Petersen and the members of nasen

Picture credits (t=top; b=bottom; c=centre; l=left; r=right;
OFC=outside front cover): Shutterstock: OFC (all), 6c, 6–7, OBC
(all). NASA/Courtesy of nasaimages.org.: 1, 2, 4, 5, 8, 9, 10, 12–13,
15, 16, 17, 18, 19 (both), 20, 21, 22–23, 24–25, 25t, 26, 27, 31.
Science Photo Library: 14. www.janespencer.com: 11, 28–29.

Every effort has been made to trace copyright holders, and
we apologize in advance for any omissions. We would be
pleased to insert the appropriate acknowledgments in any
subsequent edition of this publication.

Library and Archives Canada Cataloguing in Publication

Owen, Ruth, 1967-
          Space survival guide / Ruth Owen.

(Crabtree contact)
Includes index.
ISBN 978-0-7787-7531-7 (bound).--ISBN 978-0-7787-7553-9 (pbk.)

          1. Life support systems (Space environment)--Juvenile
literature. 2. Space flight--Physiological effect--Juvenile
literature. 3. Space suits--Juvenile literature. I. Title.
II. Series: Crabtree contact

TL1500.O94 2010   j629.47'7   C2009-906951-2

Library of Congress Cataloging-in-Publication Data

Owen, Ruth, 1967-
   Space survival guide / Ruth Owen.
      p. cm. -- (Crabtree contact)
   Includes index.
   ISBN 978-0-7787-7531-7 (reinforced lib. bd.g : alk. paper) --
   ISBN 978-0-7787-7553-9 (pbk. : alk. paper)
   1. Space suits--Juvenile literature. 2. Weightlessness--Juvenile
literature. 3. Space biology--Juvenile literature. I. Title.

TL1550.O94 2010
629.45'84--dc22
                                                   2009048070

CONTENTS

*An astronaut
during a
space walk*

CHAPTER 1

SPACE AND THE HUMAN BODY

Have you ever wondered what it is like to go into space?

What is it like to live on a space station 217.5 miles (350 kilometers) above Earth?

space shuttle launch

Astronauts have to travel, live, and work in an extreme **environment**. The human body was not designed to survive in this environment.

There is no air to breathe in space. It is so cold that the human body will freeze. Harmful rays from the Sun will burn human skin.

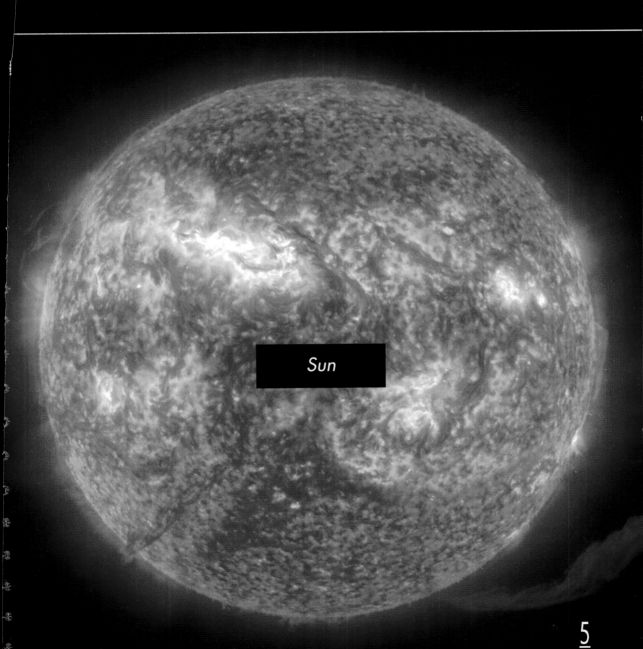

Sun

If you left a spacecraft without a space suit, you would pass out in just a few seconds. You would be dead within a minute or two.

Without air, there is no oxygen. People need to breathe oxygen to stay alive.

On Earth, air pressure provides a **force** on our bodies. In space, there is no air pressure. This means the pressure inside your body would push outward. However, there would be no outside force pushing back to balance it.

The gases in your organs would expand quickly. Your organs would swell up. Your body would become swollen. Blood would no longer be able to flow through your body.

To survive in space, astronauts must use special clothing and equipment. They must also train hard.

Could you be an astronaut?

Do you have what it takes to survive in space?

Earth

CHAPTER 2

TRAINING FOR SPACE SURVIVAL

Astronauts are trained to be experts at space survival.

As a **NASA** astronaut candidate you will take part in a one-year course. You will learn how to fly and repair a spacecraft. If something goes wrong on a spacecraft, it is up to you and your **crew** to fix it!

an astronaut during a spacecraft training session

You will also have medical training. If an astronaut is hurt or gets ill in space, the other crew members must know what to do.

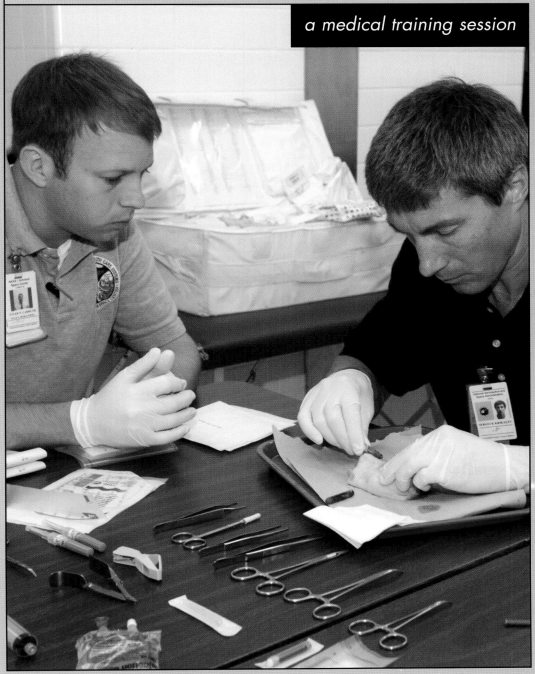

a medical training session

CHAPTER 3

SPACE SUITS FOR SURVIVAL

Sometimes you will have to leave the safety of your spacecraft. This is called a space walk or EVA (Extra-Vehicular Activity).

You will need to wear a space suit to protect yourself from the extreme environment in space.

an astronaut during an EVA

A space suit is like a small spacecraft.
The space suit has 14 different layers.

LCVG (Liquid Cooling Ventilation **Garment**)
It covers your entire body to keep your body cool. It has three layers that draw away your sweat and carry cool water.

The bladder layer keeps air pressure at the right level and holds in oxygen for breathing.

A tear-resistant layer protects the suit from damage.

There are layers of strong material to keep the bladder layer in place.

The outer layer is made of materials that can resist water, fire, and even bullets.

There are seven layers of insulation to protect you from heat and cold.

The helmet is an important part of the space suit. Oxygen flows into the helmet so you can breathe.

The helmet's visor is covered in a thin layer of gold. The gold protects you from the Sun's harmful rays.

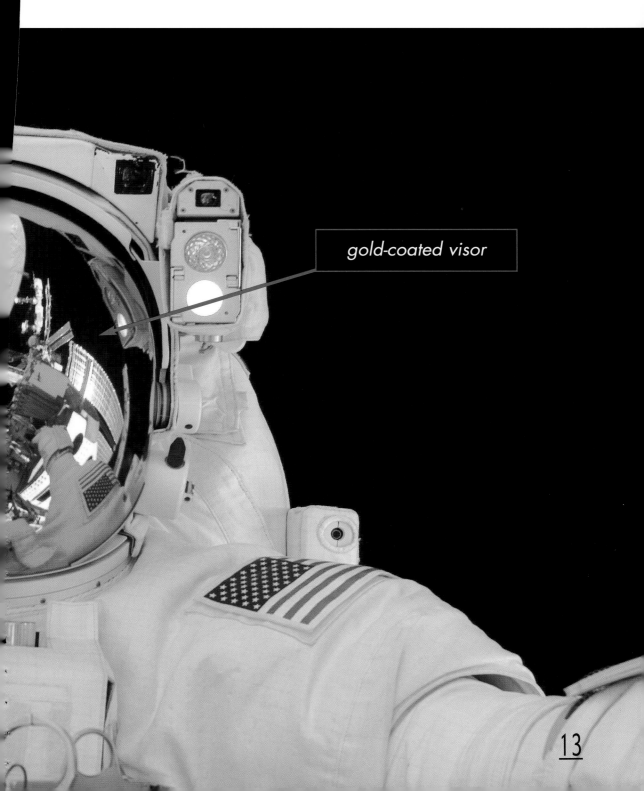

gold-coated visor

At NASA, they have many different-sized space suit pieces.

a variety of space suit sizes

Scientists will take measurements of your body. The measurements are compared to all the space suit pieces at NASA. Then, the scientists will build a suit for you. It is designed to fit you perfectly.

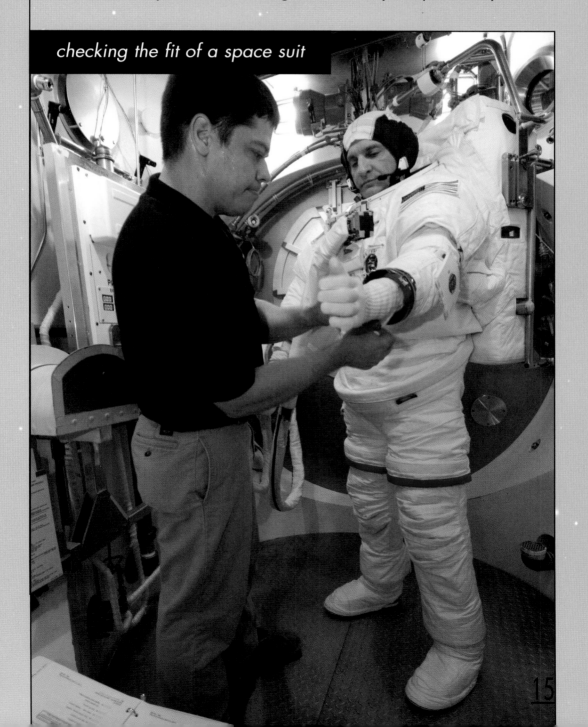

checking the fit of a space suit

CHAPTER 4

SURVIVING SPACE WALKS

Astronauts make space walks to build or repair the International Space Station (ISS).

a space walk to repair the ISS

During a space walk, you might be out in space for a long time. You could not survive without a space suit.

During a space walk, you will wear a backpack called a **Primary Life-Support** Subsystem (PLSS). The PLSS has oxygen tanks. It also removes the harmful **carbon dioxide** that you breathe out.

PLSS

During a space walk you will wear safety tethers. The safety tethers are connected to the spacecraft. The tethers stop you from floating off into space.

safety tethers

You will also wear a piece of equipment called SAFER (Simplified Aid for Extravehicular Activity Rescue). SAFER is powered by small jet thrusters. If your tethers break, you can use SAFER to fly back to the spacecraft. You will use a joystick to steer SAFER.

PLSS

SAFER

gas supply for thrusters

joystick

untethered astronaut testing the SAFER

Each mission or space walk is different. If you make a mistake, the mission could fail.

You might be chosen to go on a space walk to fix the **Hubble Space Telescope**.

During the space walk, you will be floating. This is because there is no **gravity** in space.

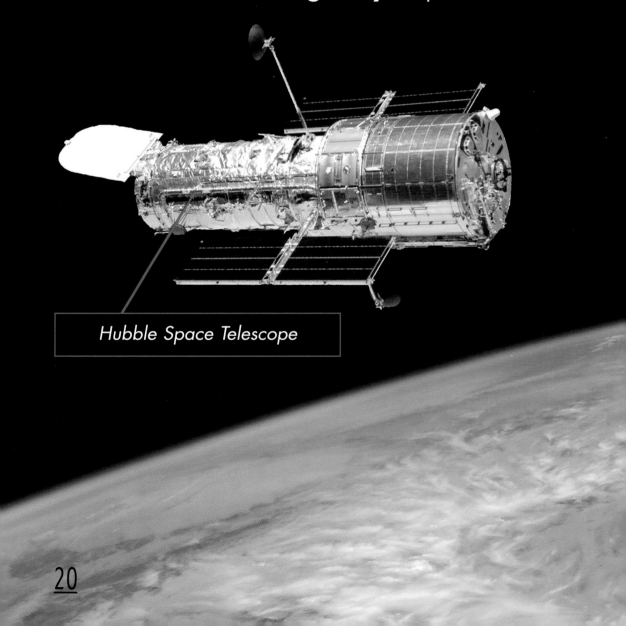

Hubble Space Telescope

You will have to carry out difficult engineering tasks. This will be very difficult when you are floating!

You will practice the mission underwater. A model of the telescope will be built in a huge tank of water. You will practice repairing the model telescope while in the water tank. Training underwater is like working without gravity in space.

underwater training

CHAPTER 5

LIVING IN SPACE

The International Space Station (ISS) is a space laboratory.

Inside the ISS, astronauts carry out experiments. Some of the experiments test how humans can survive in space.

ISS

You might be chosen for an ISS mission. You will live on the ISS for several months. The space station supplies the oxygen you will need to survive.

The oxygen is made using a process called electrolysis. Electricity is used to split water into hydrogen gas and oxygen gas. The electricity comes from the space station's **solar panels**.

solar panels

During a mission, you must eat healthy foods to keep yourself strong and fit. NASA scientists will plan your meals for each day of the mission.

Many types of food are eaten in space. Some foods are dehydrated. This means all the water has been removed. To eat these foods you just add water to the packages.

Food has to be stored securely otherwise it floats around the spacecraft due to the lack of gravity.

Your body can only survive for a few days without water. It is expensive to bring water to space from Earth. So, water is recycled on the ISS.

When you breathe or sweat this produces **water vapor**. A machine collects the vapor and turns it back into water. Even the water from your urine is recycled!

water recycling machine

a package of dehydrated food

Living without gravity weakens your bones and muscles. When you are living in space, you must exercise for two hours each day to stay strong.

There is a treadmill and exercise bike on the ISS. The exercise will keep your muscles and bones strong. If you did not exercise, you would not be able to stand up when you return to Earth!

This spacecraft version of an exercise bike is called a cycle ergometer.

exercising on a treadmill

A harness connects you to the treadmill so you do not float around.

CHAPTER 6

SURVIVING AN EMERGENCY

Astronauts fly to and from the ISS on the space shuttle. During take-offs and landings, they wear a special suit called the Advanced Crew Escape Suit.

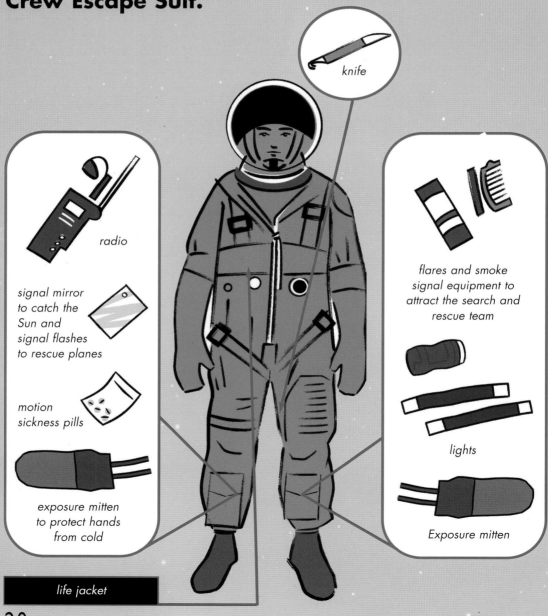

knife

radio

signal mirror to catch the Sun and signal flashes to rescue planes

motion sickness pills

exposure mitten to protect hands from cold

flares and smoke signal equipment to attract the search and rescue team

lights

Exposure mitten

life jacket

If the shuttle loses pressure, the suit will protect you. You might have to bail out over the ocean.

The suit will keep you warm. It also has a lot of survival equipment.

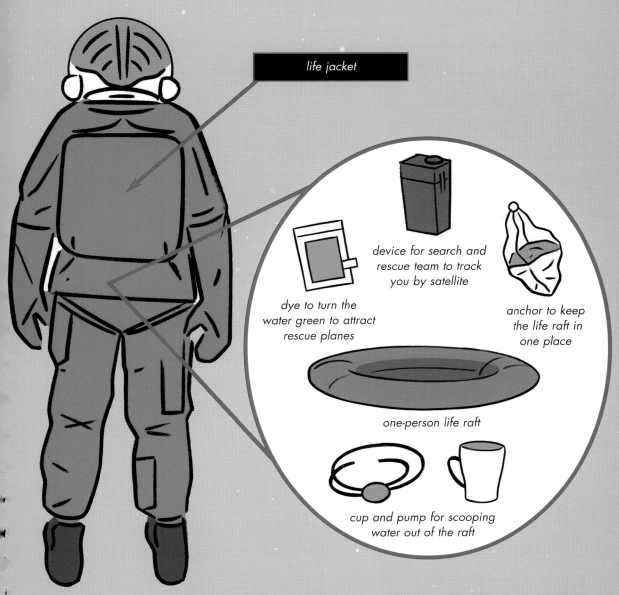

life jacket

dye to turn the water green to attract rescue planes

device for search and rescue team to track you by satellite

anchor to keep the life raft in one place

one-person life raft

cup and pump for scooping water out of the raft

NEED-TO-KNOW WORDS

carbon dioxide A gas that humans and animals breathe out

crew The group of people who work on a space shuttle, airplane, ship, or train

environment Your surroundings

force The scientific term for push

garment A piece of clothing

gravity The force that holds us onto Earth

Hubble Space Telescope A telescope that orbits Earth and sends back images from outside of Earth's solar system

International Space Station (ISS) A space laboratory that was built by the United States, Canada, Russia, Japan, and several European countries

laboratory A room or building where scientific experiments are carried out

life support Something that keeps a body alive

NASA The National Aeronautics and Space Administration is an organization in the United States that is in charge of U.S. space travel and study

primary First or most important

solar panel A piece of equipment that uses the Sun's power to produce electricity

water vapour A mass of tiny water droplets that look like mist

MORE SPACE SUIT FACTS...

- Some space suits are plain white. Others have red stripes or candy cane stripes. The different designs help the crew identify the person inside the suit.

- It takes an astronaut around 45 minutes to put on a space suit.

- An astronaut's fingers get very cold in space. The space suit gloves have heaters in the fingertips.

space suit with a candy cane stripe

SPACE ONLINE

Find out how often astronauts change their pants in space!
*www.nasa.gov/audience/forstudents/k-4/stories/
no-washers-dryers-in-space.html*

Read about living in space with the European Space Agency.
www.esa.int/esaKIDSen/Livinginspace.html

Learn about the space shuttle launches and other events from NASA's video gallery.
www.nasa.gov/multimedia/videogallery/index.html

View the NASA online "book" of everything to do with space.
www.nasa.gov/worldbook/

INDEX